BREAKING

SATANIC
STRONGHOLDS

HOW TO LIVE IN FREEDOM FROM OPPRESSION AND
MOVE FORWARD IN THE THINGS OF GOD

DR. RUTH W. SMITH

BREAKING

SATANIC
STRONGHOLDS

HOW TO LIVE IN FREEDOM FROM OPPRESSION AND
MOVE FORWARD IN THE THINGS OF GOD

DR. RUTH W. SMITH

MEWE
Lithonia, GA

Publisher: MEWE, LLC
Lithonia, GA
www.mewellc.com

Breaking Satanic Strongholds
First Edition
ISBN: 979-8-9871970-1-1

For Worldwide Distribution

Printed in the USA

DEDICATION

To God the Father, God the Son, God the Holy Spirit, my beautiful children, including all my seed, the Body of Christ, Light of the World Christian Tabernacle International, Light of the World Covenant Fellowship International, and all of humanity that God so loved that He gave His Son to die for and His Spirit as a constant companion.

May we purpose to be alert and break every satanic stronghold using our AUTHORITY IN CHRIST JESUS.

TABLE OF CONTENT

INTRODUCTION

Breaking satanic strongholds is critically important if we want to live in total freedom from oppression and move forward in the things of God. You can be sure that satan and his demonic forces are all around, waiting for any chance to invade our territory and set up strongholds in our lives. Ever since he deceived Adam and Eve, satan has been preying on humankind to sow his seeds in the minds of believers and non-believers alike.

Now, since satan is a spirit, he has to have a human host to operate in and manifest his nature. In other words, he has to find a willing vessel to cooperate with him and be used for his purposes. Nobody is exempt from his reach. Each of us has some kind of a weakness or vulnerability that he can exploit. That is why we must be aware, ready, and alert. To do so, we must understand how this kind of warfare is waged; otherwise, we are trapped in his schemes and may not even know what happened. There is hope, and it is found in the Word of God.

- Dr. Ruth W. Smith

The Nature of Strongholds

So, let us first understand what a stronghold is. The Bible describes a stronghold as a fortress, a place of refuge, and protection from our enemies.

In Psalm 18:2 (NIV), David, running from his enemies, says that God is his stronghold:

> ***The LORD is my rock, my fortress and my deliverer; my God is my rock, in whom I take refuge, my shield and the horn of my salvation, my stronghold.***

We must make God our stronghold in order to protect us from our spiritual enemy, satan. But strongholds can also be demonic. These are places in our lives that are controlled by the enemy to hold us tight within his grip and constrain us. This is the meaning of strongholds ascribed by Paul in 2 Corinthians 10:4-5 (NIV, emphasis added):

> ***The weapons we fight with are not weapons of the world. On the contrary, they have divine power to demolish strongholds. We demolish arguments and every pretension that sets itself up against the knowledge of God, and we take captive every thought to make it obedient to Christ.***

Strongholds, in the Greek context, imply resistance and barriers to knowing the truth. These barriers are largely arguments, thoughts, and opinions formed in us that are contrary to the word of God. Why are they formed? Their intent is to hinder the move of God in us and to restrict us from submitting to the will of God and progressing in spiritual things.

Normally, when we use the term "mind," we are referring, in a general way, to our will, our intellect, and our emotions – our human nature. But we often forget that we are primarily spirit beings as seen in 1 Thessalonians 5:23, *"May God himself, the God of peace, sanctify you through and through. May your whole spirit, soul and body be kept blameless at the coming of our Lord Jesus Christ."* As spirit beings, we are connected with God and can communicate directly with Him spirit to Spirit. This is largely through interacting with His Word. Knowing the truth has never been more crucial than at a time when we are fed with so much disinformation from the world's system. We must therefore not be gullible to opinions that are outside of the Bible and pray for strong discernment to separate truth from error.

Above all, we need to understand that we are fighting an invisible foe, not people. When we find ourselves putting a human name or face to a situation we are going through, we're likely to miss the power of God. No, our battle is not with people; it's with the spirit of the enemy that's trying to penetrate our mind.

How does the enemy penetrate our mind? He attacks an area of weakness or vulnerability, slipping through the cracks in our spiritual armor in the same way a burglar enters our home when we forget to lock the front door. Satan cannot really force his way into your mind. No, we have to give him an entry point to come in and set up camp.

To know which area in our mind we have opened, we must start by admitting we all have weaknesses. We have to identify these weaknesses, and make sure that we have accountability over them. Our accountability is to the Word of God, which acts like a two-edged sword and exposes every hidden thought and motive (See Hebrews 4:12). Without accountability, we may think our way is right, but it only leads to destruction (See Proverbs 14:12).

Accountability comes from studying the word, but it also comes in the form of counselors or accountability partners who can keep us in check. The Bible says in the multitude of counselors there is wisdom (See Proverbs 15:22). Why do you need a multitude of counselors? Sometimes you need different perspectives. Sometimes you need to hear things that are not palatable to you and have someone brave and loving enough to tell you. And, even if you believe God is still talking to you, you need discerning counselors who can either agree with you or point out your error.

As our loving Father and Protector, God will never let you walk into a blind avenue without warning. He will always reveal the dangers lurking in the shadows of our own weaknesses. In Proverbs 7, we see the example of the young man walking into the territory of the harlot to clearly show us the danger of giving in to illicit sexual pleasures. This is a warning to all of us not to be so easily led into a trap and to stay away from the seductions of the flesh. And, just as the young man who – not so innocently – walks into the harlot's domain and is snared, once we give into our weakness, we give access to satan to enter and build a stronghold.

You may be aware of some persistent sin or habit in you, such as watching pornography or hanging out in certain company. You know that you want to get rid of it – you want to quit, you want to change, but, somehow, you just don't seem to be able to shake it off. That's because a stronghold is already forming within you.

One common entry point is disobedience. Once we open that door by intentionally disobeying what the Word of God says, satan has a right to come in and take root. That satanic spirit then mobilizes its forces to infiltrate your mind. What is more challenging is that he reinforces a stronghold with the occupation of a strongman.

What Is a Strongman?

A strongman is a dominant spirit that rules all the other spirits that could have taken up residence within you. It could be a strongman of lust, or covetousness, or anger that can control your whole personality and compel you to act without restraint in certain circumstances. Once there is a strongman spirit in your house, it is very difficult to break free from its grip. You cannot evict it on your own and need help.

We first see the strongman exposed by Jesus in Luke 11:21-22 (NIV):

> *When a strong man, fully armed, guards his own house, his possessions are safe. But when someone stronger attacks and overpowers him, he takes away the armor in which the man trusted and divides up his plunder.*

In this context, the devil, himself, is the strongman, fully armed with his secret weapons of deception and all his fake armor that his victim covers themselves in. We have to get help to unlock that door to let that strongman out. And that's why, when we sit in our disobedience, our pride, and our self-righteousness, and pretend we're not bound by a stronghold, we remain captive. As we refuse to acknowledge its presence, our condition only gets worse. We have to be willing to humble ourselves at the altar of God, and let people pray through on our behalf to cast out that spirit from us.

But no one can cast off the spirit if we will not admit it is on us, and if we do not genuinely want to be set free. Yes, we want to quit smoking, but only after the next puff. God is not going to violate our will and force us to be rid of it. We have to be willing vessels to want the liberty for which Jesus Christ has already paid such a great price. His death and resurrection have already set us free, but we must stand on that victory in the name of Jesus. God is not going to force you; He only gives you the opportunity to find that freedom.

So, in due course, that stronghold is reinforced by the presence of the strongman, and now it becomes a bondage. Do you see how we get deeper and deeper into it? You can always see it working on our carnality, through lustful thoughts, anger, rage, greed, or deception – as we shall soon see when we examine Galatians 5. That is why you have to slam the door shut the minute you see the enemy creeping in on you. When things are being put in your ear, when you sense that subliminal messages are being sent across to your spirit through the television or music, you have to shut that door.

It is not enough to mentally reject those thoughts or feelings. You have to renounce them in the atmosphere – that is, in the spirit realm. You must tell the principalities and powers that you reject those thoughts and impulses. If you do not release the truth for yourself, with your own mouth, what was imparted will take root in your soul. Jesus showed us that the words we release through our mouth are spirit and they are life (See John 6:32). Therefore, our words have power against the demonic realm.

Using Our Spiritual Weapons

We can try to use our human will to remove the strongman or spirit of bondage upon us. But the word of God says that our battle cannot be won by fleshly means, only by God's way. That is why we have to use our spiritual weapons. When we try to fight the battle our way, we open ourselves to self-righteousness, because now, we are ruling with our minds. Self-righteousness allows the spirit of pride to take over. The strongman is still in control, and the spirit of bondage is entrenched. What are the weapons of our warfare?

For though we walk in the flesh, we do not war according to the flesh. For the weapons of our warfare are not carnal, but they are mighty through God, in God, for the pulling down of strongholds. Casting down arguments and every high thing that exalts itself against the knowledge of God, bringing every thought into captivity to the obedience of Christ (2 Corinthians 10:3-5 NKJV).

Note that verse 5 emphasizes that the method of our warfare is not in obedience to the flesh or our carnal mind: it's in obedience to Christ. When you submit your mind, heart, and soul to Him and dismantle your wrong thinking, He will deliver you from those strongholds.

Now the question is how do we tell the difference between the principles of the world system and the principles of the Kingdom? All things that are contrary to the Kingdom principles taught by Jesus in Matthew 5 are the principles of the world.

Anything operating outside of the plan of God, or the way God fights is not of God. It's a dog-eat-dog world out there, governed by lawlessness, fleshly desires, striving, and deception. The world does not fight fair, but we don't have to live or fight our battles that way.

Now when you look at the church and also see unprincipled things happening, that means it's operating by the world system, not the Kingdom system. When you operate according to godly principles, all of us can work together. But if we work out of worldly principles, then there's carnality, strife, and division. This should not be so in the house of God.

So, the weapons of our warfare are for demolishing that entire massively corrupt culture we live in. We use our power for God, to smash warped philosophies, tear down barriers erected against the truth of God, and fit any loose thoughts, emotions, and impulses into the structure of life shaped by Christ. Our tools are ready at hand for clearing every obstruction and building lives of obedience into maturity. That is the goal.

How Strongholds Begin

Strongholds do not happen overnight; they begin from small habits. We have already discovered that satan first looks for our weakness and uses it as ammunition against us. Then he locates the vulnerable areas of our life: difficult situation, character flaws, past failures, etc. Those are the areas he targets, shooting his fiery darts of temptation.

A stronghold begins to be set up when we give satan permission to enter our lives through disobedience and permit him to have control. That's why it is so important to obey God. We have to refuse to submit to the flesh or be moved by our emotions just because we're angry. We have to refuse to allow ourselves to be manipulated by others just because they are influential. We have to learn to recognize satan's tactics. For example, the Bible says satan is the accuser of the brethren (See Revelation 12:10). So, if you sense an accusing spirit whispering in your ear pointing at people, that is a sign satan is talking to you. That spirit is *resting* on people who like to criticize, judge, accuse, and backbite.

Because satan is the god of this world, he has the legal right to influence and harass us. The *Fall* gave him that right. If we give him access, he will do just that – influence and harass us. And remember this important fact: God will grant satan's petition (as we see with Job) if no one contests.

So, if you're trying to understand how satan managed to worm his way into your life, it's because there was no contest when the devil started to influence you. You didn't put up a fight and chase him off. You didn't stop watching that movie, reading that magazine, or ceasing from that idle chat on social media. You gave him room to infiltrate. But it's not too late to repent and come out of it.

Now some of us would disagree with the notion that believers can sin. We would argue that, because we are born again, we do not sin anymore. That is a distortion of what the Word really says. It is true, we are new creations in Christ and do not have the nature of sin, but we still have freedom of choice. We all stumble and fall, and we often miss the mark, which is sin. The Bible says if we say we do not sin, we deceive ourselves and make God a liar (See 1 John 1:8, 10). No, we have to continually bring ourselves before God for Him to shine His light in us and cleanse us. When we are honest with ourselves and come clean, He's just waiting to bless us.

So don't just quote one scripture without balancing it with the whole counsel of God. Make sure you listen to what God is saying, looking into the lens of truth to always see God's will. Sometimes, we work against God unwittingly through our misconceptions.

Examples of Strongholds

Now that we understand how strongholds begin, we will look at examples of strongholds. A good classification can be found in Galatians 5 where Paul exposes the works of the flesh.

> *The acts of the flesh are obvious: sexual immorality, impurity and debauchery; idolatry and witchcraft; hatred, discord, jealousy, fits of rage, selfish ambition, dissensions, factions and envy; drunkenness, orgies, and the like. I warn you, as I did before, that those who live like this will not inherit the kingdom of God* (Galatians 5:19-21 NIV).

Sexual sins

The first group consists of sexual sins like masturbation, rape, prostitution, homosexuality, fornication, adultery, sexual abuse of children, and pedophilia. To this, we could include pornography and sexual fantasies. In the first place, if you are single, you should not be having sex.

Don't be fooled by what your peers are doing around you or be convinced by them. You can be single and still live a holy life and not be persuaded to think that it is unnatural not to be sexually active.

On the other hand, there are husbands and wives, who, though married to each other, are just roommates. They are not intimate with their partner. If you are not behaving as a married couple, you open the door for satan to enter and lure you into sin.

Spirit of revelry

The next category is the spirit of revelry: drinking, partying, night clubbing, and we can add to the list other addictive behaviors such as smoking and using drugs as well as compulsive eating – they all lead you deeper into strongholds.

Witchcraft

The third category is idolatry and witchcraft. This is not just about blatant worship of idols or occult practices but also of hero-worshiping a person (a movie star perhaps) or idolizing one's own opinions above the Word of God. Any opinion that we hold on to which is contrary to the Word of God is a form of idolatry, and so is entertaining fears or phobias, unbelief, negative imaging, or indulging in vain imaginations such as living in a fantasy world.

We could also be using manipulative behavior in a relationship – which is no different than witchcraft. Even having unhealthy soul ties becomes a form of witchcraft. Sexual promiscuity often leads to ungodly soul ties, which need to be severed. If an individual's mother dies and the person continues to grieve for years after that, that's an evil soul tie at work, which could lead to sin.

Works of the flesh

The last category, works of the flesh, is rooted in the spirit of anger: hatred, discord, jealousy, fits of rage, selfish ambition, dissensions, factions, and envy. They stem from malice, envy towards others, and selfishness. We can include in this category anything that violates the rights of another – stealing, lying, corruption, slander, gossip and malice.

Works of the flesh start at the individual level and escalates to hatred of a community, people or group, and may lead to public acts of violence, riots and revolts against the state. Sometimes all that needs to happen is to take offense at something, and the devil can use that as fertile ground to sow seeds of discord.

In Genesis 4, the Bible tells how Cain was offended because his offering was considered unworthy, while his brother Abel's was accepted. Rather than resolve that issue with God, he let his offense brew in him, and in no time that bitter root grew into a poisonous tree, ending in murder. Now, while slander is prohibited, it doesn't mean you go to the other extreme and not speak up for the truth when you see injustice. If you saw some public wrongdoing that affected the helpless such as cheating or lying and you exposed that wrongdoing, that is your biblical duty. If you see satan at work in the education system polluting the minds of the young, then it's time to be vocal and act. Does not the word of God command us to *"speak the truth in love"* (Ephesians 4:15)? However, many times God's people are fearful of speaking up against the system for fear of reprisal. It is the devil at work trying to shut the mouths of the saints when they speak the truth and turn people against them.

Characteristics of Strongholds

The next thing we want to understand is recognizing strongholds on people's lives. Strongholds can differ greatly from each other, but they do have certain common characteristics.

Stubborn

First, strongholds are stubborn. They seem impossible to get rid of. Notice I said, "seem" because they are not impossible to pull down if they are confronted in the right way. We must again take heed of the warning that strongholds cannot be pulled down by a person's own human efforts or through religious activity. They will soon form again if we attempt to take them down on our own without God's help.

Irrational

Number two, strongholds are irrational because the person has little control over them once they are established. Somebody that is under the control of a stronghold can be logical at times but at other times there are so many gaps and inconsistencies in their reasoning, they don't make sense. Do not entertain that kind of irrational communication. I love the scripture that says, ***"Don't answer the foolish arguments of fools, or you will become as foolish as they are."*** (Proverbs 26:4 NLT). That's why you have to be silent in some conversations. Do not waste your breath defending your position, or arguing, or trying to explain – do not even attempt to clarify the truth. Let the lie pass without saying a word.

As the scripture says, if you try to reason with a fool, then you are going to look like one, too. Anyone from the outside looking at two people head-to-head in an argument is not going to tell which one is the fool!

Uncontrollable

People with strongholds are – well, uncontrollable. They refuse to be corrected, disciplined, or to be guided by good sense. They simply speak their mind without restraint, not realizing that this in itself reveals a stronghold.

Most times strongholds develop from simple behaviors that go unchecked, like telling white lies or losing one's temper. A pattern of behavior can become a habit and, before you know it, you're subject to feelings of depression, out of control mood swings, temper tantrums, lying and compulsive behavior of all types. The stronghold has become a way of life for you and a recognizable part of your personality.

Counterproductive

Strongholds are also counterproductive. Some things we do with the intention of alleviating our hurt can only bring more pain to us, and we're worse off than before.

Demolishing Strongholds

Sometimes, we're in denial because we've bought into the lie that a Christian cannot be oppressed by demons. The reality is that a born-again believer is not exempt from such a condition. Unless the believer is filled with the Holy Spirit and cleansed by the word, demons can invade his personality and will stubbornly resist any attempt to evict them.

Identify the stronghold

So how do we pull down and demolish a stronghold? The first thing to do is to identify the stronghold and admit we have it. Until we are willing to admit our condition and receive help, we cannot be set free. Even when we are delivered, we have to maintain our freedom and not give room for satan to harass us again. Jesus' warning in Luke 11:24-26 (NKJV) is highly relevant to deliverance:

> *When an unclean spirit goes out of a man, he goes through dry places, seeking rest; and finding none, he says, 'I will return to my house from which I came.' And when he comes, he finds it swept and put in order. Then he goes and takes with him seven other spirits more wicked than himself, and they enter and dwell there; and the last state of that man is worse than the first.*

Why is the house empty? Because it is not occupied by the things of God. Nature never tolerates a vacuum and, soon enough, the house is re-visited by the same tenant: that evil spirit bringing with him more wicked spirits.

Take authority

Secondly, we have to take authority over the intruder. As we saw in Mark 3:27, *"No one can enter a strong*

man's house and plunder his goods, unless he first bind
the strong man, and then he will plunder his house." So,
you use your authority in Christ Jesus, and bind that
strongman – of lust, violence, false religion, or deception.
You can't just gloss over it. You demolish all false
arguments with the truth of the Word and reason, just as
Jesus did with the slanderous words of the enemy.

And the enemy is not partial to whom he uses. Notice
how he used religious scholars from Jerusalem to spread
rumors that Jesus was working black magic through, the
prince of devils, Beelzebub – satan himself, *"He hath*
Beelzebub, and by the prince of the devils casteth he out
devils" (Mark 3:20). They were accusing the Son of God
of using the devil's tricks to impress people with His
spiritual power. Jesus confronted that slander with sound
reasoning:

> *How can Satan cast out Satan? If a kingdom is*
> *divided against itself, that kingdom cannot stand.*
> *And if a house is divided against itself, that house*
> *cannot stand. And if Satan has risen up against*
> *himself, and is divided, he cannot stand, but has*
> *an end. No one can enter a strong man's house*
> *and plunder his goods, unless he first binds the*
> *strong man. And then he will plunder his house*
> *(Mark 3:23-27 NKJV).*

To rephrase the last line, "How is it possible to enter the house of an awake, able-bodied man in broad daylight and walk out with his possessions? No, you have to first tie him up. Once he's tied up, then you can clean out the house."

Intercede

The third strategy is intercession. Intercession is so critical to our warfare. It starts by standing in the gap for people. In Matthew 17:14-20 (NIV), we find the disciples frustrated because they were unable to cast a demon out of a young boy. They had cast out demons before, but this one was very resistant. Jesus rebuked the demon, it came out, and the boy was healed immediately.

> *Then the disciples came to Jesus in private and asked, "Why couldn't we drive it out?" He replied, "Because you have so little faith. Truly I tell you, if you have faith as small as a mustard seed, you can say to this mountain, 'Move from here to there,' and it will move. Nothing will be impossible for you."*

Walk in faith

This is a faith walk, people of God. If you have faith, you can move mountains.

Now, we often think that this type of deliverance only happens with fasting and prayer. But what Jesus was actually saying was that the only way you can summon the faith for this kind of deliverance is through fasting and prayer. Jesus was really talking about faith, not deliverance.

So don't get to delivering people too fast, especially if they are not prepared. You've got to fast and pray to build up your faith. It is all about faith. If you can believe, you can have it. But now, remember, the kingdom operates according to principles and here we can consider the principle of "line upon line, precept upon precept" (See Isaiah 28:10). So, you can't just start naming and claiming, while going *against* the Word, truth, and righteousness; and thinking that if you can believe it, you can have it. That's trying to manipulate the Word, which is akin to witchcraft.

The simple truth is that if you have a mere kernel of faith, you will tell the mountain, move, and it will move. There is nothing you wouldn't be able to tackle. Now, you have to know who you are in Christ, and you have to walk in truth to exercise your faith like that. This deliverance is available for us. Jesus has already given it to us. It is already yours. It is not something you have to qualify for if you are already a child of God. You are righteous because of what Jesus did for you. And then, if you walk in faith, God will take away the fleshly issues that you are dealing with on your Christian journey.

CONCLUSION

In conclusion, the overriding principle in pulling down strongholds is displacement. This is how you pull down strongholds: you've got to displace them. We need to separate ourselves from that which is vile and unclean and no longer be tied to them:

> **Do not be unequally yoked together with unbelievers. For what fellowship has righteousness with lawlessness? And what communion has light with darkness? (2 Corinthians 6:14 NKJV)**

The message is: Do not become partners or associates with those who reject God. How can you make a partnership out of light and darkness or right and wrong? That's not partnership, that's war. Can the light – God, Jesus, and the truth – be best friends with darkness? Does Christ go strolling with the devil? Do trust and mistrust hold hands? Who would think of setting up a pagan idol in God's holy temple? That is exactly what we are: His holy temple, a temple in whom God lives. God Himself put it this way: "I live in them, move in them. I will be their God, and they will be My people" (See Jeremiah 32:38).

"So, leave the corruption and compromise. Leave it for good," says the Lord. "Don't continue to have fellowship with those who will pollute you. I want you all for Myself." If you are able to give God all of you, you have to line up with every principle in God's word. He'll be a Father to you, and you will be His sons and daughters.

I pray for everyone who has a stronghold and desires to be set free. The only condition is that you are willing to do what it takes to be delivered, and you're ready to stand firm in this liberty. So, invite the presence of God once again into your life, invite the Spirit of God to fill you, and open yourself up to the truth of God's word without any compromise. Then watch and see the power of God at work – instantly or progressively – to deliver you and set you free.

ABOUT THE AUTHOR

Dr. Ruth W. Smith, a native of Greensboro, Alabama, accepted Christ in 1964 and was filled with the Holy Spirit in 1981. She married Pastor Jimmie Lee Smith in 1982. Answering the call to the ministry in 1990, she co-founded Light of the World Christian Tabernacle International and Light of the World Covenant Fellowship International and was later ordained as a minister in 1991. Under the dynamic leadership of Pastors Jimmie Lee and Ruth W. Smith, The Light grew from 400 to 1,500 members in a 4-year period. In 2008, Archbishop Jimmie Lee Smith went home to be with the Lord, and the stirring vision of the ministry to "see a world without darkness" continued.

Light of the World Covenant Fellowship International is an organization that mentors and empowers Pastors and Ministries throughout the world. Dr. Ruth was consecrated Archbishop of the organization on July 13, 2008 and became the first woman to receive the title of Archbishop and serve a worldwide Diocese, overseeing ministries in 26 countries with a membership of over 200,000.

Dr. Ruth's passion for helping people advance the Kingdom of God started from an early age when she participated in the integration of schools in Hale County, Alabama. Through her leadership at The Light, she champions community support through food and clothing drives. In 2013, she received the "Torch Bearer" award by the Southern Christian Leadership Conference (SCLC) in Washington, DC, in recognition of her many years of work as a scholar and spiritual leader committed to the legacy of SCLC founder, Dr. Martin Luther King, Jr.

She recently opened the Jimmie Lee Smith Community Center (JLSCC), which provides Sports, Education and Entertainment to the surrounding communities. Additionally, she established three SateLight locations: LOTW Decatur, December 2015; LOTW South, April 2016; and LOTW Gwinnett, December 2016.

Dr. Ruth holds a Master's degree in Biblical Counseling and a Doctorate in Ministry from Biblical Life College and Seminary in Marshfield, Missouri. She is the published author of six other books, *A Word on Love*, *Keep Moving*, *Rules of Encouragement*, *The Voice*, *Generosity Is the Heart of God*, and *Greater Is Coming*.

She is the proud mother of five children, twelve grandchildren and four great-grandchildren, whom she dearly loves. She is anointed to preach and teach the gospel of Jesus Christ, which she does readily worldwide. Her foundational gifts are administration and governments, and her foundational scripture is Romans 8:28, *"For we know that all things work together for good to them that love God, to them who are the called according to His purpose."*

CONTACT INFORMATION

Ministry
Light of the World Christian Ministries
5883 Highway 155 North
Stockbridge, GA 30281
678.565.7001
thelight@comeintothelight.org
www.comeintothelight.org

Purchasing
678.565.7001
www.comeintothelight.org

Publisher
MEWE, LLC
404.482.3135
mewecorporation@gmail.com
www.mewellc.com

www.ingramcontent.com/pod-product-compliance
Lightning Source LLC
Chambersburg PA
CBHW021005150626
46549CB00012BA/1344

* 9 7 9 8 9 8 7 1 9 7 0 1 1 *